The Story of

Musical Notes

IN DIE NATIUITATIS DÑI

STÃ AD SCM PETRI M-

P UER NATUS EST NOBIS

Ps Cantare dño 11 ADR. Nomm ſeetꝛ

RG Viderunt om   nes fineſ ter

rae ſalutare   de   2 noſtri

iubilate deo om niſ   ter

riꝰ.   V̄ Notum ſecit

do   mi

niſ ſalutꝰ   re ſuum ante

conſpectum gentium re uela uit

iuſti tiam ſuam.

Alleluia

IN DIE NATIVITATIS DÑI

STẢ AD SCM̃ PETRI M~

P VER NATV̄ EST NOBIS

Ps Cantate dño ɑɑ ẢDR· Nomñ seɑr

RG Viderūm om̄ ines fineſ ter

rae ſalutare de ɑ noſtri

iubilate deo om niſ ter

riſ V̄ Noɑūm ſecꝛt

oo mɑ́

miſ ſalutɑ re ſuum anɑe

conſpectum gentiūm re uela uri

ɑutu tram ſuam.

ẢLLĹẎIẢ

The Story of

Musical Notes

By JEAN CRAIG

Illustrated by GEORGE OVERLIE

Prepared under the supervision of Robert W. Surplus

Musical Books for Young People

LERNER PUBLICATIONS COMPANY
MINNEAPOLIS, MINNESOTA

International Copyright Secured. Printed in U.S.A.

Library of Congress Catalog Card Number: 62-18819

Second Printing 1963
Third Printing 1964
Fourth Printing 1965
Fifth Printing 1966
Sixth Printing 1967
Seventh Printing 1968

CONTENTS

AMERICA

Samuel Smith   Henry Carey

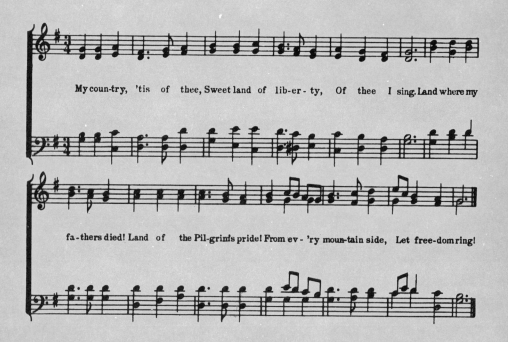

My coun-try, 'tis of thee, Sweet land of lib-er-ty, Of thee I sing. Land where my

fa-thers died! Land of the Pil-grim's pride! From ev-'ry moun-tain side, Let free-dom ring!

4

Our Way of Writing Music

Suppose that you knew a song, and that you wanted to teach it to a friend. How would you go about it? If you were both in the same place, you could teach it by singing or playing it over and over until your friend had learned it.

But what if your friend lived in a different city? You could send him the music for the song, and if he knew how to read the music, he would soon be able to sing or play the song as well as you.

If the song were the one printed on page four, what would your friend be able to tell by looking at it? By knowing what each printed sign meant, he would be able to tell the two things a person needs to know in order to play or sing a piece of music. He must know just how high or low each note is— the *pitch* of the note. He must also know how long each pitch is to be held —the *rhythm* of the music.

The signs that tell about the pitch are, first of all, the *staff* and the *notes*. A staff is made when five lines are drawn across a page. Where a note is placed on the staff tells the pitch of that note. If the round part of the note, called the *note head*, is on a higher line or space of the staff,

the note stands for a higher pitch. If the note head is on a lower line or space of the staff,

the note stands for a lower pitch.

When notes are placed on a staff, they are given names which are the first seven letters of the alphabet.

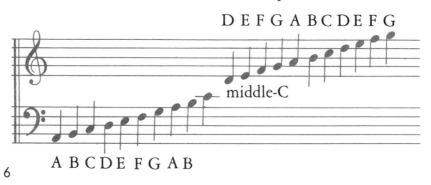

Another sign that tells about pitch is the *clef*. The curly arm on the *G-clef* or *treble clef*

wraps itself around the second lowest line of the staff, and shows that any note on that line

is called "G". The two dots of the *F-clef* or *bass clef*

are above and below the fourth line from the bottom of the staff, and show that any note on that line

is called "F".

A third sign that tells about pitch is the *key signature*. In this piece the key signature is one sharp. This means that all

f's in the piece are to be raised to f#.

The last sign that tells about pitch is the *accidental* (ak-si-DEN-tul), which is the sharp added in the fourth measure of the bottom line.

This sign raises the d to d# for the rest of that measure.

You will notice that for the word "My" in the song, there are four notes. The top note is called the *melody* note. If you were to sing the melody note for each word or syllable, people would be able to tell that you were singing *America*. The other three notes under each melody note are the *harmony notes*. If you had three friends sing the harmony parts while you sang the melody, *America* would sound much richer and fuller. That is what harmony does for a melody.

The melody part is often called the *soprano* part. Soprano comes from a word meaning highest. The part below the soprano is called the *alto* part. The higher part on the staff below the words is called the *tenor* part, and the part below that, the *bass* part.

The length each pitch is to be held can be told by the way in which the note is made. We can show how long each note in *America* is by drawing lines under the words and notes of the piece. The longer the line, the longer the note is to be held.

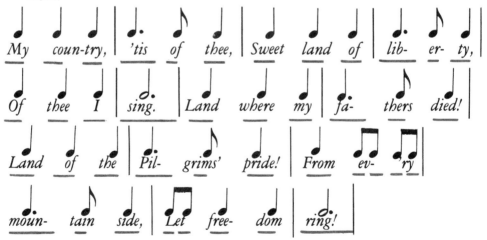

You can see that the lines under the first three notes are exactly the same length. The three notes are also made in the same way. These three notes are called *quarter notes,* and get one beat each. The line under the word " 'tis" is a little longer. The note for this word is called a *dotted quarter note,* and gets a beat-and-a-half. The line under the word "of" is quite short. The note for this word has a flag and is called an *eighth note.* An eighth note gets only half a beat. The notes above the third word from the end, "Let", are also eighth notes. Eighth notes may be written either way—each note with a flag, 𝅘𝅥𝅮𝅘𝅥𝅮 or barred or fastened together 𝅘𝅥𝅮𝅘𝅥𝅮 . The line under the word "ring" is three times as long as the line under the word "My". The note is a *dotted half note* and gets three beats.

There are two other signs that help with the rhythm of the music. One sign is the *bar line.* Bar-lines are the up-and-down lines that divide this piece into *measures.*

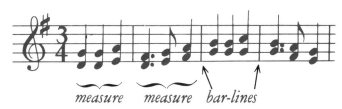

measure   measure   bar-lines

The other sign is the *time signature,* in this piece 3/4. This means that in *America* there are three beats in a measure, and that a quarter note gets a beat.

Earliest Ways of Writing Music

With our system of notation (our way of writing music), your friend would not need to hear the piece first before being able to play or sing it. This was not so, many centuries ago. In the early days of the Christian Church, melodies used in the services were memorized by the singers. It became impossible for the singers to remember the many melodies that were used, as more were added.

The words of the melodies sung by the singers were written out by hand by men called *scribes*. About the fifth century, scribes began to help the singers by marking hints of the melody above the words. If the melody went up, the scribe would write a short line going up ╱ . If the melody went down, he would write a line going down ╲ . If the melody went down, then up, he would use a combination of both signs ╲╱. These signs, called *heighted neumes* (newms), were used only as hints to remind the singers of the general direction of the melody which they had already learned.

Today we would have a great deal of trouble trying to tell the melody just from these neumes, because each scribe would copy the neumes a little differently from another scribe. There is no way of telling just how high or low a neume meant the melody to go. If there were a skip in the melody, there was no way of telling how wide the skip was. Neumes had nothing to do with the rhythm of the melody. Such melodies were *chanted,* that is, the rhythm of the melody followed the rhythm of the words much as they were spoken.

During the eighth century, some scribe drew a red line and placed an "f" at the beginning of the line. Any sign on the line stood for the f below middle-c.

Any sign above the line stood for a higher pitch than f, any sign below for a lower note. Still later, someone else added a yellow line above the red one. The yellow line stood for middle-c. The two lines helped to make music much easier to read, but it still was almost impossible to sing a piece of music from this type of notation without hearing it first.

If you were forced to use the notation of this period to teach your friend *America*, it would look somewhat like this:

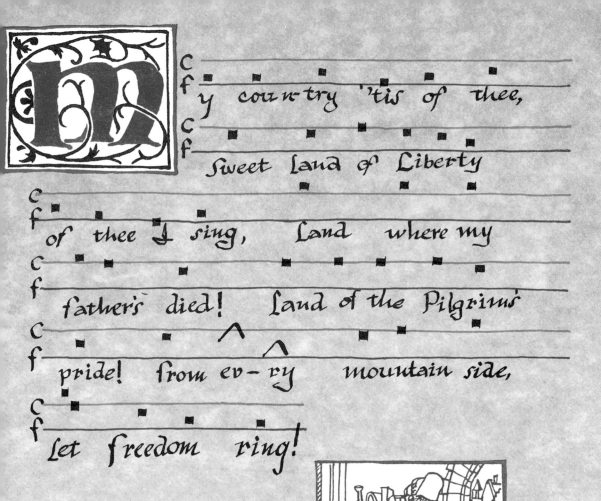

My coun-try 'tis of thee,

Sweet land of Liberty

of thee I sing, Land where my

father's died! Land of the Pilgrims

pride! from ev-ry mountain side,

Let freedom ring!

The mark for the pitch of the first word in *America* is just above the red line. This means that the first pitch is the g below middle-c,

insead of the g used for the first word in our example of *America* in modern notation.

This makes no difference in the way it would be sung. People with higher voices would naturally start on the g above middle-c because the higher note would be much more comfortable for them.

This is the same as when a man with a low voice sings the melody to *America* from modern notation. He would not be comfortable starting on the g above middle-c, and therefore would start on a lower g.

A performer would be able to understand some things by looking at *America* in *neumatic notation* (new-MĂ-tik), meaning music written using neumes. Other things are missing that we think necessary in order to sing or play a piece of music. First of all, just the melody would be performed without any harmony. At the time neumatic notation was in use, harmony was just beginning to be used, and it was very difficult to write it down.

14

There is no time signature in this music because neumes did not show rhythm. There is no key signature in this notation either. The performers were expected to change the music to make it sound like the scales they were used to hearing. It would be up to the performer to sharp all the f's in the music. A performer would be able to tell the correct pitches in the melody fairly well, as long as the music did not go too far above or below the red and yellow lines.

If there were only one pitch on each syllable, a point or dot was used to show the pitch, as in the first two lines of *America*. If there happened to be more than one note on a syllable, as in the word "ev'ry" in the third line, a special type of neume was used. The sign used for the word "ev'ry" is called a *clivis* (KLEE-vis) ⌒ , and stands for two pitches, the second being lower than the first. There were many other neumes that were used for more than one note on a syllable. One was the *pes* (pace) ∪ , which stood for two notes, the second being higher than the first. Others were the *scandicus* (SKAN-di-koos) ⸱⸱∕ , which stood for three rising notes, the *climacus* (KLEE-ma-koos) ∕⸲ , which stood for three notes going down, and the *torculus* (TOR-koo-lus) ⌒∙ , which stood for three notes, with the middle one higher than the first and third notes.

There were other attempts at developing a clearer notation. One system that developed during the ninth century used something that looks like our staff. Only the spaces in the staff were used, instead of both the lines and spaces as in our system. The words of the melody were written in the spaces.

America would look somewhat like this in this type of notation:

My coun-try, 'tis of thee, Sweet land of

li-ber-ty, of thee I sing. Land where

my fa-thers died! Land of the Pil-grims'

pride! From e-v-r-y moun-tain side

Let free-dom ring!

Each space stood for a certain pitch, and was separated from the next higher or lower space by a line marked with an "S" or a "T". The S stood for *semitone,* and meant that the lines marked "S" separated pitches a half-step apart. A half-step is the distance from one note to the note closest to it. You can find examples of how a half-step looks on a piano keyboard in the chart below. The T stood for *tone,* and meant that the lines marked with a T separated pitches a whole-step apart. A whole-step is two half-steps. You can find examples of how a whole-step looks on this chart.

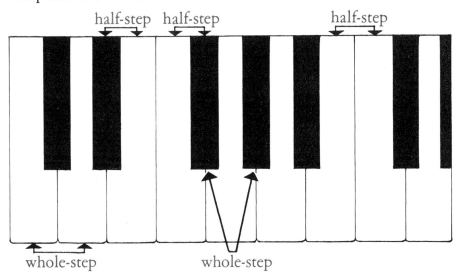

This system of notation was certainly better than neumatic notation in showing exact pitches. It still did not show the rhythm of the melody. It was also not a good system if a melody had a wide range. If the melody went too high or too low, a great many lines were needed. Too many lines make music reading difficult, and confuse the performer.

America looks like this in Gregorian notation:

Y country tis of thee, Sweet

land of liberty, Of thee I sing. Land where my

Fathers died, land of the Pilgrim's pride, from

ev-ry mountain side, let freedom ring!

Square Notes and Gregorian Notation

Most musicians feel that a man named Guido d'Arezzo did more for music notation than any other person. He was an Italian monk who lived during the eleventh century. Guido is given credit for the final development of the four-line staff which is still used for notating the chants of the Catholic Church. As these chants are called *Gregorian chants,* this notation is called *Gregorian notation.*

This type of music was copied by scribes who decorated the initial of the first word. This type of decoration was called *illumination.* Many museums have examples of illuminated manuscripts.

A square mark was used to show the pitch of a note in Gregorian notation. As in neumatic notation, the rhythm of a melody was not shown, although pitches with dots after them were held longer than other notes. The words were sung in much the same rhythm as they were spoken.

The big forward step with Gregorian notation was that each pitch was given its own line or space on the four-line staff. There was still no key signature, and singers were expected to add a sharp or flat when one was needed. When there was more than one pitch on a syllable, as in "ev'ry", special signs were used called *ligatures* (LIG-a-choors). These put together two or more pitches. They are not hard to understand if you look at them carefully. The small sign at the end of each line shows the pitch of the first note on the next line. This sign is called a *custos* (KOO-stus).

America looks like this
in white notation.

Diamond Notes and White Notation

Gregorian notation was fine for chanted church music, as long as the melody stayed mostly within the range of the staff. But what if the melody had a wide range? Instrumental music, music without words to help with the rhythm, was becoming more and more important. This created a need for some way of notating rhythm. And what of harmony parts? It was possible to write a second or even a third part on separate *staves* (more than one staff). But if this were done, how could the singers tell which harmony notes went with which melody notes without some way of counting beats?

During the fifteenth and sixteenth centuries, these problems were solved with a type of notation which is the father of our own system. This type of notation is called *white notation*—that is, most of the notes were "white" or not filled in in the center. It is like our system because performers could tell how long to hold notes by the way they were made.

There are many signs in this notation that look very familiar to us. First of all, we can recognize our five-line staff. For many years, musicians had experimented with staves of different numbers of lines. By the time white notation was developed, the five-line staff was used in most places. It had enough lines to allow a fairly wide range in the music written on it, yet it did not have so many lines that it confused the eye of the performer.

The first sign on the staff looks a great deal like our G-clef. In fact it is a G-clef when it still looked like the letter "G".

There is still no key signature. At the time white notation was in use, the only key signature that was used much was one flat. A key signature of more than one flat was thought to confuse the performer. If a composer needed more than one flat, he would flat the notes he wished within the music instead of in the key signature. Key signatures with sharps were not used yet. Any sharps that were needed were added within the piece. You will notice that the sharp before the fourth note looks like our sharp sign, except that it is turned on its side and is like a double-x.

The circle after the G-clef is a kind of time signature. Although white notation used no bar-lines and measures, this piece divides naturally into sections of three beats each. To a person living in the fifteenth or sixteenth century, three was the "perfect" number. When a piece of music divided into sections of three beats, a "perfect" figure was used to show this at the beginning of the piece. The circle was thought to be the perfect figure because a circle has no beginning and no end. When a piece divided into sections of two or four beats, an "imperfect" figure was used—a broken circle C . We still use this figure in our music for 4/4 time.

At the end of each line you will see a wavy line with a tail. This sign is called a *custos* or a *director.* It is the same as the *custos* in Gregorian notation. It serves as a guide to the performer by showing him the pitch of the first note on the following line. This sign was used in music until after 1750. The *custos* was used in the music of Johann Sebastian Bach (1685-1750), and was still used during the lifetime of Wolfgang Amadeus Mozart (1756-1791).

Harmony parts were still not written on the same staff as the melody as in our music. When harmony parts were written, they were often printed in this way on two pages of a book:

Music was printed this way so that the music book could be placed on a table, and the four performers could stand on either side to sing the piece. More than one part was written on a staff during the sixteenth century, but then only for keyboard (harpsichord, clavichord, or organ) music.

Notice the clef sign in the bass part.

 F

It looks very much like our F-clef except that it has been placed on the third line of the staff. In notation of this period, clefs were *movable*—they could be moved to any line of the staff. All the other notes on the staff would move too, of course.

The alto and tenor parts use the C-clef. In the tenor part, middle-c is on the middle line of the staff.

 C

In the alto part, middle-c is on the lowest line of the staff.

 C

In this type of notation, what we think of as being very long notes in our system, were held for a very short time. The first three notes in our example of *America* in white notation look like our whole notes. This type of note is called a *semibreve* and receives one beat in perfect time. The fourth note is a dotted semibreve and receives a beat-and-a-half. The fifth

26

note is a *minim* (MĬ-nim) and gets half a beat. The last note is a *breve* (breev) and receives three beats in perfect time.

From this white notation, it was an easy step to our modern notation. The following chart shows what each note or rest in white notation is equal to in our notation.

WHITE NOTATION			MODERN NOTATION		
	Note	Rest		Note	Rest
Large	▭	‖			
Long	▭					
Breve	▭	▬			
Semibreve	◇	▬	Whole Note	𝅝	▬
Minim	♩	▬	Half Note	𝅗𝅥	▬
Crotchet (KRAH-chet)	♩	𝄽	Quarter Note	♩	𝄽
Quaver	♪	𝄾	Eighth Note	♪	𝄾
Semiquaver	♬	𝄿	Sixteenth Note	♬	𝄿

The bar-line was introduced during the last part of the sixteenth century in vocal music. It had already been in use for a century in instrumental music. The bar-line is a help to the eye, and makes it possible for the performer to keep his place more easily.

Once the problems of notating rhythm and pitch were solved, the last stage in the development of musical notation took place. Composers began using additional signs to tell the performer how they wished their music to be played. One type of sign, called a *dynamic* (die-NA-mik) *sign*, tells how loudly or softly the composer wishes the performer to play. Dynamic signs range from *fortissimo* (for-TISS-i-mo) which means "as loudly as possible", to *pianissimo* (pe-an-ISS-i-mo) which means "as softly as possible". Other signs have to do with the *tempo* (TEM-po) or speed of the music. They range from *largo* (LAR-go) or slowly, to *prestissimo* (pres-TISS-i-mo) or as quickly as possible. Tempo and dynamic markings are usually in Italian, and every musician knows what they mean no matter what country he lives in. Still other signs are written above or below the notes in a piece of music. One is the dot which means to play a note *staccato* (stuh-CAH-to), meaning separated. Another, the *accent* (ACK-sent) mark $>$, means to stress the note, and a third, the *fermata* (fur-MAH-tuh) ⌒, means to hold a note longer than its written value.

Syllables, a Help to Singers

Earlier in this book, in the part about Gregorian notation, we spoke of a man named Guido d'Arezzo. Guido did a great deal for music besides developing the four-line staff. He also invented the system of syllables that we still use today.

Guido had a choir that sang for the services in his church. Part of his job was to teach the boys in the choir to read music. One of his biggest problems was to teach his students how pitches were *related*—that is, if the choir sang the first pitch of a melody, how high or how low they were to sing the next pitch.

Guido had noticed that in a Latin hymn to Saint John the Baptist each phrase began on a higher pitch. This is the hymn:

The Latin words mean: "Oh holy John, remove all stain of sin from our lips, that with relaxed throats we may sing of your wonderful deeds."

Guido took the first pitch and syllable of the first six phrases. This made six notes of a scale.

ut, re, mi, fa sol la

Later, in France and Italy, the syllable *ut* (oot) was changed to *do*, and *si* or *ti* was added as a seventh syllable. This gave us our complete scale of syllables—*do, re, mi, fa, sol* (or *so*), *la, ti, do.*

This is the way in which these syllables help the singer. When the singer is given a melody to sing, he finds the pitch in that melody which is *do*. Once he finds *do*, he can name all the other pitches in the melody. He can also be sure that each step up the scale of the melody is a whole-step except for *mi* to *fa*, and *ti* to *do*, which are half-steps. Knowing where the half and whole-steps are makes it possible to sing the melody correctly.

31

AMERICA

| d | :d :r | t₁ | :—.d : r | m | :m :f | m | :—.r :d |

| d | :d :r | t_1 | :—.d : r | m | :m :f | m | :—.r :d |
| s_1 | :s_1 :l_1 | s_1 | :—.l_1: t_1 | d | :d :d | d | :—.t_1 :l_1 |

My coun-try, 'tis of thee, Sweet land of lib- er- ty,

| m | :m :f | r | :—.r : s | s | :l :l | s | :—.f : m |
| d | :d :f_1 | s_1 | :—.s_1: s_1 | d | :l_1 : f_1 | s_1 | :—.si_1: l |

| r | :d :t_1 | d:—:— | s | :s :s | s | :—.f :m |
| l_1 | :s_1 :s_1 | s_1:—:— | m | :d :m | m | :—.r :d |

Of thee I sing. Land where my fa- thers died!

| f | :m :r | m:—:— | s | :s :s | s | :—.s :s |
| f_1 | :s_1 :s_1 | d:—:— | d | :m :s | d | :—.d :d |

| f | :f :f | f | :—.m :r | m | :f.m :r.d |
| r | :r :r | r | :—.d :t_1 | d | :d :d |

Land of the Pil- grims' pride! From ev- 'ry

| ṣ | :s :s | s | :—.s :s | s | :l.s :f.m |
| s_1 | :t_1 :r | s_1 | :—.s_1 :s_1 | d | :d :d |

| m | :—.f: s | l.f | :m :r | d:—:— |
| d | :—.t_1: d | d | :d :t_1 | d:—:— |

moun- tain side, Let free- dom ring!

| s | :—.s: s | f.l | :s :f | m:—:— |
| d | :—.r: m | f | :s :s_1 | d:—:— |

Syllables have been a great help to music teachers in teaching the reading of music. In Wales, they have proved to be so valuable, that they are used many times *instead* of notes! *America* written out in the manner of some Welsh hymn books would look like the sample on page thirty two.

The letters stand for the first letters in the syllables—"d" for *do,* "r" for *re,* "m" for *mi,* "f" for *fa,* "s" for *so,* "l" for *la,* and "t" for *ti.* Look at the top or melody line. Can you follow the tune of *America* in this notation? In Welsh hymn books, the tunes were written out in this notation using both melody and harmony parts. The soprano and alto parts were written above the words, the tenor and bass parts below the words.

In this way of writing music, each measure was divided into beats by a colon (:). In the first measure, each note gets one beat, so the notes are separated by colons.

$$| \quad d \quad :d \quad :r \, |$$

My   coun - try

The note in the last measure gets three beats. This is shown by putting dashes between the colons, which means that the note on the first beat is held through the second and third beats.

$$| \, d \, :— \quad :— \, \|$$

ring!

For the word "ev'ry" each beat is divided in half by a period to show that two notes are sung for each beat.

$$| \quad m \quad :f.m \, :r.d \, |$$

From ev - ry

In the second measure,

$$| \, t_1 \quad :—.d \quad :r \, |$$

'tis of thee

the note for the word " 'tis" lasts past the first beat. This is shown by the dash after the colon followed by a period. The word "of" starts in the second half of the second beat—after the period. The number one to the lower right of the note for the word "'tis" means that the pitch of that note is below *do*.

Can you see what is missing from this way of writing music that was in all our other examples? In our other examples, it was easy to tell whether the pitches in the melody went up or down by the position of the notes on the page. High pitches *looked* high, and low pitches *looked* low. In this notation, a performer must know that *re* is higher than *do* in order to sing the first three notes. He cannot tell by the picture of the notes how high or low the pitches are.

America

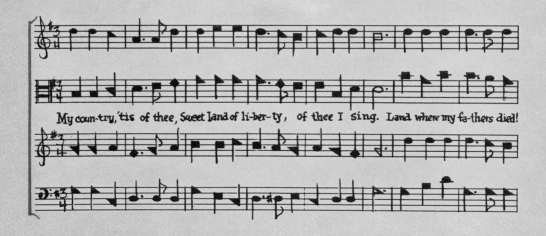

My coun-try,'tis of thee, Sweet land of li-ber-ty, of thee I sing. Land where my fa-thers died!

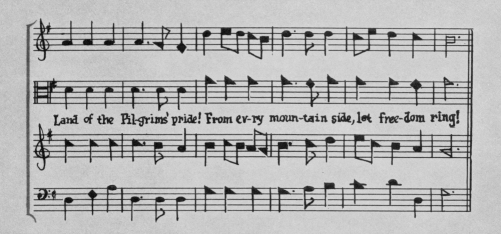

Land of the Pil-grims' pride! From ev-ry moun-tain side, let free-dom ring!

America looks like this in buckwheat notation.

Fasola and Buckwheat Notation

In parts of England by the sixteenth century, many people did not use all the syllables. Instead of singing a scale *do, re, mi, fa, so, la, ti, do,* they sang it *fa, so, la, fa, so, la, mi, fa.* Singing was taught in many schools using the *fa-so-la* scale. Having more than one *fa, so,* or *la* did not seem to confuse anyone. During the eighteenth century, the fasola scale was brought to this country where it was used in "singing schools" taught by singing teachers who traveled from town to town.

About 1800, note shapes were invented for the fasola system. A triangle was used for *fa* ◢ , a regular, round note for *so* ♩ , a square note for *la* ♩ , and a diamond-shaped note for *mi* ◆ . These differently shaped notes were called "patent" notes by the people who used them, and "buckwheat" notes by people who poked fun at them.

In some books printed in buckwheat notation, the melody was in the tenor, or higher men's part. So in our example, the melody to *America* is in the tenor part, the part on the third staff. In this kind of notation, the melody was not given to women's voices until about 1845.

You can see that buckwheat notation looks almost exactly like our own notation except for the shape of the note head. The notes are placed on the staff just as we place them in our notation, and the rhythm is written exactly as we would write it.

Are the buckwheat notes really helpful? In this example, we can already tell the pitch of the note and the shape of the melody by where the notes are on the staff. We can tell the length of the note by how it is made. The different shapes of the note heads add very little, and might help to confuse some people. Helpful or not, buckwheat notation was used well into the twentieth century in parts of the United States.

About 1830, someone went so far as to print a hymn book using seven shapes instead of four, one for each of the seven syllables. The G-scale in seven-shape notation looks like this:

Seven-shape notation was not used very much because each book printed with this notation had a different set of shapes. Some of the shapes used were: ⌐ ⌛ ℂ ⌐

There were other experiments in notation, using numbers, letters, and even numbers inside the note heads. All these experiments tried to replace Guido's seven syllables. One man even got so tired of all these different "systems" of reading music that he suggested, as a joke, a scale using animals.

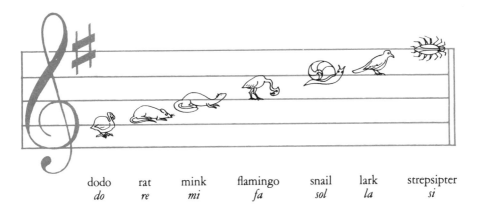

	dodo	rat	mink	flamingo	snail	lark	strepsipter
	do	*re*	*mi*	*fa*	*sol*	*la*	*si*

A Closing Note

We have taken a look at some of the systems that have been used to write down music. The system we use is the best because it shows most clearly the two things we need to know in order to perform a piece of music. It gives a picture of how the melody goes, and how long the notes are to be held.

Our system is not perfect, for no notation can completely capture all the feelings of the composer. These feelings can only be supplied by a skillful performer. The notes on a page are only signs, and music does not exist until it is heard.

In tracing the development of musical notation, a simple piece of music known by all young people has been used. In order to introduce the young reader to notation of music, and to focus his attention upon those aspects of the musical score that are necessary for good reading of music, we have used this familiar melody for illustration. The author and editor are fully aware that a large portion of the early music in our western civilization was chanted, and that music with such strong rhythmic emphasis as in *America* was not a major part of the musical scene.

ABOUT THE AUTHOR

Jean Craig is a native of Cleveland, Ohio. Her early musical training was at the Cleveland Music School Settlement, where she studied violin, piano, and music theory. She is a graduate of the Oberlin Conservatory of Music, with a degree in music education. For the past four years, Miss Craig has taught music in the Cedar Rapids, Iowa public schools. She also plays in the Cedar Rapids Symphony Orchestra and teaches violin and flute privately. Currently she is enrolled as a graduate student in music and music education at Teachers College, Columbia University.

STÃ AD SCÃM PETRI M-

A PUER NATVS EST NOBIS

Ps Cantare dño ii ADR · Nomm̃ secr̃

RG Viderũt om̃ nes fines ter

rae salutare de i nostri

iubilate deo om̃ nis ter

riu V Notum fecit

DO mi

nus salutã re suum ante

conspectum gentium reuela uit

iusti tiam suam.

ALLELVIA

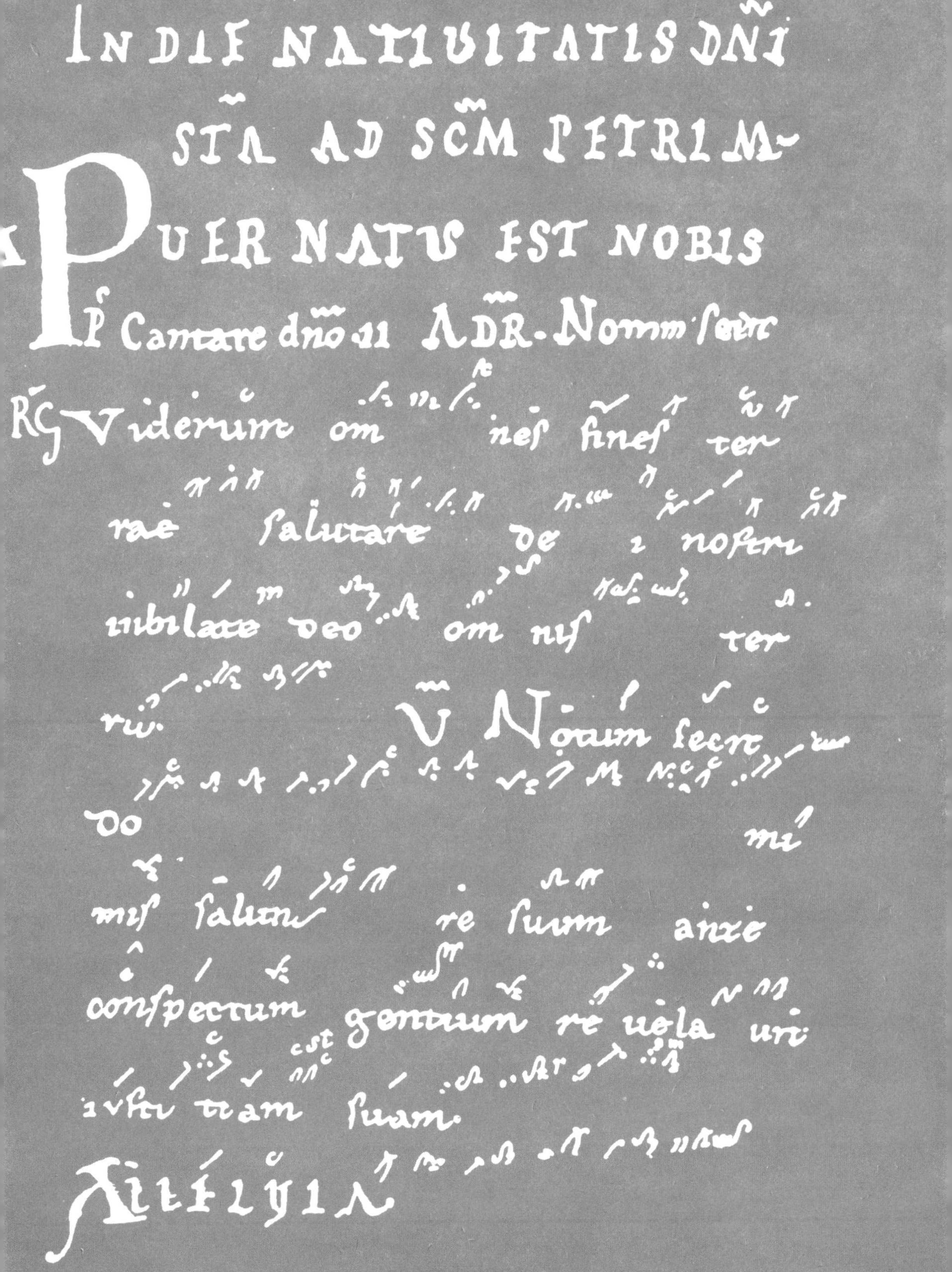

STA AD SCM PETRIM

P UER NATU EST NOBIS

P Cantate dño ii ADR. Nomm feert

RG Viderunt om ines fines ter

rae salutare de nostri

iubilate deo om nis ter

ra.

V Notum feert

do mi

nus saluta re suum ante

conspectum gentium re uela uri

iustitiam suam.

ALLELYIA

We specialize in publishing quality books for
young people. For a complete list please write

LERNER PUBLICATIONS COMPANY

241 First Avenue North, Minneapolis, Minnesota 55401